T0297486

The Story of the Day You Were Born

Denise Burroughs

Illustrations by Jingo M. de la Rosa

© 2012 Denise Burroughs. All rights reserved.

No part of this book may be reproduced, stored in a retrieval system, or
transmitted by any means without the written permission of the author.

AuthorHouse™
1663 Liberty Drive
Bloomington, IN 47403
www.authorhouse.com
Phone: 833-262-8899

Because of the dynamic nature of the Internet, any web addresses or links contained in this book may have changed
since publication and may no longer be valid. The views expressed in this work are solely those of the author and do not
necessarily reflect the views of the publisher, and the publisher hereby disclaims any responsibility for them.

This book is printed on acid-free paper.

ISBN: 978-1-4772-4547-7 (sc)
ISBN: 978-1-4772-6496-6 (e)

Library of Congress Control Number: 2012912625

Print information available on the last page.

Published by AuthorHouse 02/19/2021

authorHOUSE®

This book is dedicated to my grandbaby Kale. You have brought so much joy, love, and happiness into my life.

Love always,

Gigi

My Unborn Child

You are not yet born and we don't
know if a boy or girl you'll be.
But each day that passes you grow closer to me.

I wonder who you'll look like, your mommy or your dad.
It doesn't really matter though; you
have already made us glad.

Each passing day I think of you, I wait, hope, and pray,

For all good things and happiness that life may bring your way.

I cannot promise beauty, wisdom, or great wealth

My greatest wish for you, my sweet
child, is only for good health.

On this very special day, the day you were born,

The angels came together and greeted
sweet beautiful wonderful you.

Oh, they left nothing out on how special you would be.

It took nine months for you to grow big and strong

So you could make your journey into the world.

Each day that passed, you grew bigger and bigger.
You stayed nice and warm nestled in your mommy's belly
As you awaited the day you would be born.

You listened to the gentle sound of your mommy's heartbeat.
It was like sweet music to your ears.

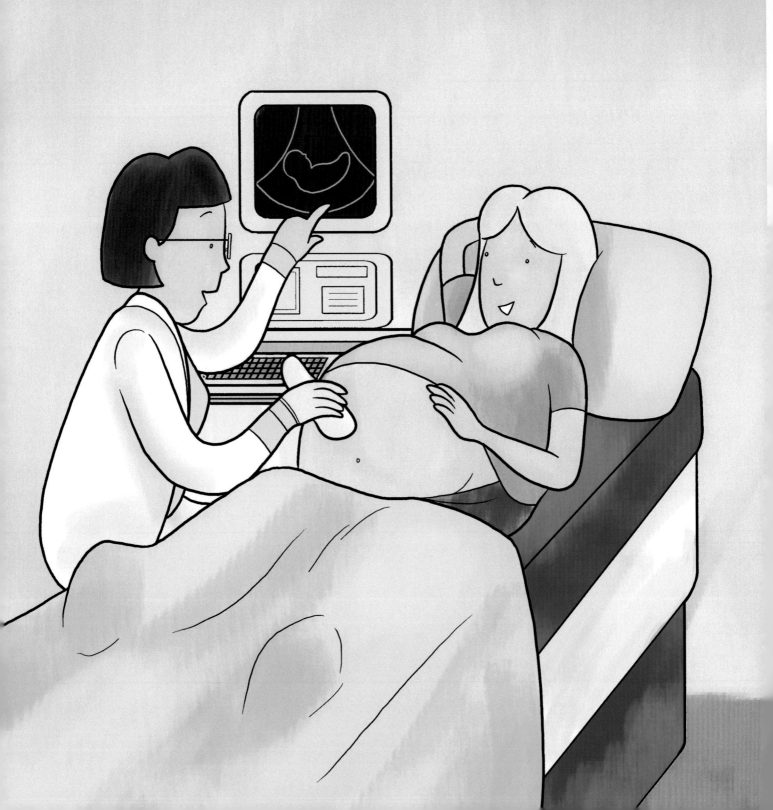

Your mommy carried you and cared for you each day until you were finished growing inside her and would make your way into the world that awaited you.

There were many visits to the doctor for you and your mommy to check on you to see how you were doing.

On some visits your mommy got to see pictures of you in her belly and even got to hear your little heartbeat.

Finally the doctor picked your birthday, so that everyone would know when to expect your arrival.

It was such a happy time for your soon-to-be family and every day brought you closer to that special day.

You continued to grow and grow; you got stronger and bigger each day. Finally, your big day was here! Your birthday, and what a joyful day it would be.

Your mommy and daddy went to the hospital to see the doctor that would help you into the world.

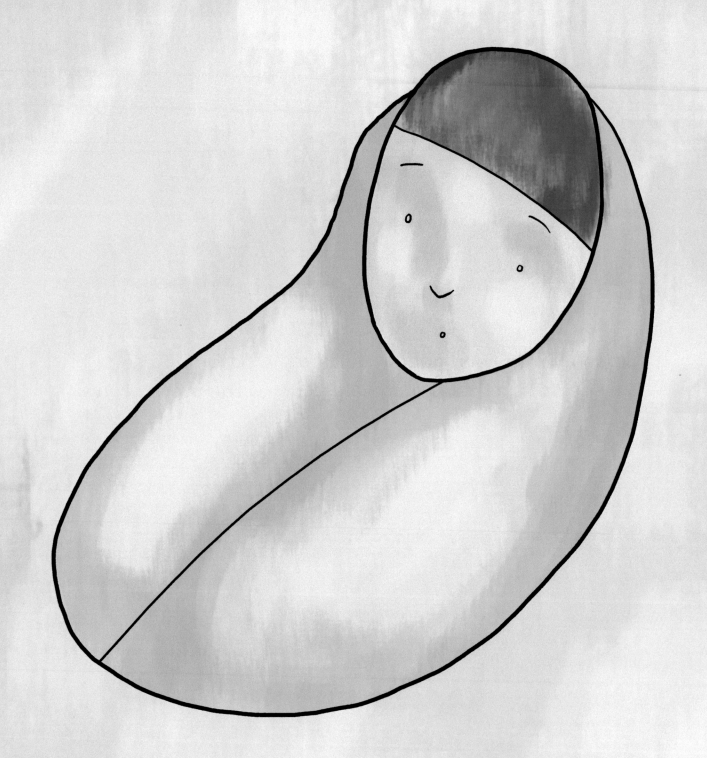

After a very long wait you were finally here. Your cry was loud but a very happy sound to your parents.

The nurse quickly got you ready to meet your new family. She washed you and wrapped you in a warm blanket and put a little hat on your head to keep you warm.

Then, with not a moment to spare, you met your mommy for the very first time. It was love at first sight. She held you close and looked deep into your eyes and kissed you gently on your face.

At that very moment you knew that everything would be ok.

There were so many people that waited to see
you and meet you for the very first time,
but all you wanted to do was sleep.

There were so many pictures taken of you on your big
day, you were like a movie star - and you were.

This is how you became you, and how you made your way into the world. This was your birthday, a day you will celebrate for the rest of your life. The day you were born.

We all have a birthday, a mommy and a daddy. For the rest of your life they will share in all your wonderful moments and teach you so very much about life, love and family.

They are your family and they love you so very much. So many wonderful things await you as you grow.

This is the day you were born.
A happy day
A special day
All about you, sweet wonderful YOU.

The End

Acknowledgements

I would like to say thank you to a few people out there for all of their support and kind words as I was writing this book. To my friends and family, thank you from the bottom of my heart, for always being there for me. To my photographer, Elliott Mccaskill with ERMPhotography for the beautiful photo on the rear cover of the book. And without a doubt to my daughter Kari. Because of you this beautiful child Kale was born, who inspired this book that was solely dedicated to him.

Printed in the United States
By Bookmasters